SUPER STARS!
SPELLING
Activity Book

ARCTURUS

ARCTURUS

This edition published in 2019 by Arcturus Publishing Limited
26/27 Bickels Yard, 151–153 Bermondsey Street,
London SE1 3HA

Copyright © Arcturus Holdings Limited

All rights reserved. No part of this publication may be reproduced, stored in
a retrieval system, or transmitted, in any form or by any means, electronic,
mechanical, photocopying, recording or otherwise, without prior written
permission in accordance with the provisions of the Copyright Act 1956 (as
amended). Any person or persons who do any unauthorised act in relation to
this publication may be liable
to criminal prosecution and civil claims for damages.

Written by Penny Worms
Illustrated by Natasha Rimmington
Designed by Graham Rich Design
Edited by Sebastian Rydberg
Consultant: Amanda Rock

ISBN: 978-1-78950-520-7
CH007254NT
Supplier 29, Date 1019, Print Run 8359

Printed in China

Parents' guide

There is more to spelling than letters and sounds. Learning phonics is a start, but to become good at spelling, your child also needs to recognize spelling patterns and high-frequency words. High-frequency words are the most common words, such as "the" and "but." Some words, like "b-u-t," can be decoded using phonics, but the tricky words, like "the," need to be learned by sight. This will help your child's reading fluency. Longer words need different strategies, such as segmenting, breaking words into syllables, and spotting compound words.

Useful words

blending	when two or more letters blend so well together that they sound like one unit of sound	"tr" as in train "st" as in stick
contraction	two words that are shortened to one, with an apostrophe representing the missing letters	it's can't
compound words	when two words join together to make one word	bedroom playground
digraph	two letters making one sound	"th" "ch"
grapheme	the letter or letters that match a sound	the grapheme for the sound "f" could be "f," "ff," or "ph"
homophones	words that sound the same but are spelled differently	hear/here
phoneme	a unit of sound	"a" in ant
segmenting	breaking a word down into phonemes or units of sound	the units of sound in dog and ship are "d-o-g" and "sh-i-p"
suffix	letter groups that are added to the ends of words to make different words	"ing" "est"
syllables	the beats you can hear in a spoken word, where each beat has a vowel	ba-na-na chil-dren
trigraph	three letters making one sound	"igh" "ear"

Sound it out

There are 26 letters in the English alphabet. Five are vowels and the rest are consonants. Here are the vowels:

a e i o u

Alphabet bricks

Write the five vowels in the alphabet grid. What sound does each letter make?

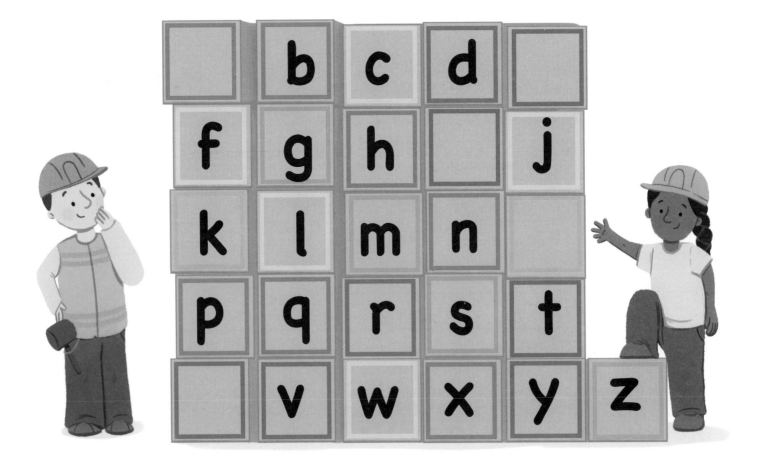

Picture crossword

Every word below has a vowel sound. Use the pictures to help you complete the crosswords.

e

y a

o

i

u n

By the sea

Read the words below and draw lines from each word to the right picture.

fish   ship   crab   ball   sun

5

Tricky words

You find the vowels "a" and "i" in a lot of words,
but they are also words on their own.

The word a

How many times can you find the word "a" in this sentence?

A dog and a cat lived in a house on a hill.

What is that?

Write "a" or "an" to complete this picture.
If the word begins with a vowel use "an."

___ eye

___ nose

___ mouth

___ ear

___ cheek

The word I

You use the word "I" as a capital letter when talking about yourself.
Write "I" in the missing spaces in this poem.

When __ walk down the street,

__ never think about my feet.

__ sometimes wonder how they know

where it is __ want to go.

The k sound

At the beginning of words, "c" and "k" can make the same sound.

c as in cake   k for kite

The king's castle

Help Egbert to his throne by following the correct spellings.

krown

crown

cing

king

kloak

cloak

kar

car

castle

kastle

Watch out!

The vowels "a" and "o" sound different after "w."
Read and underline the correct spellings.

wasp
wosp

wond
wand

worm
werm

watch
wotch

werld
world

Tricky, tricky

The word "was" is a tricky word. It sounds like "woz." Write it in this poem.

When I _ _ _ one, I learned to run.

When I _ _ _ two, I went to the zoo.

When I _ _ _ three, I learned ABC.

When I _ _ _ four, I learned lots more!

Word endings

Look out for the "f," "l," "s," "z," and "k" sounds at the end of words.
Sometimes, the spellings aren't the same as they sound.

f becomes ff, as in cli<u>ff</u>   l becomes ll, as in we<u>ll</u>

s becomes ss, as in ki<u>ss</u>   z becomes zz, as in bu<u>zz</u>

k becomes ck, as in du<u>ck</u>

Duck's truck

There are four spelling mistakes in this poem.
Underline them when you find them.

Here is Duck in his pik-up truck.

The truck is stuk in mud and muk.

They don't have much luc,

Duck and his truck.

Write the correct spellings here:

10 ------   -----   ----   ----

Double letters

Can you make real words by writing in "ff," "ll," "ss," or "zz" at the end?

The "a" sound changes when followed by "ll."

cli__

we__

a__

ki__

o__

bu__

dre__

Tricky words

The words below are spelled as they sound, and do not need extra letters.
Write them in the sentences listed and read them out loud.

| if | us | bus | Yes |

I will push __ you pull.

Look at __!

The boy missed the ____.

Do cows give us milk? ___!

11

Sight words

Learning these words will really help you with your reading.
Read each one, say it out loud, cover it up, and then write it in the sentence.

big   The dog is _____.

him   Can I pet _____?

his   Is that _____ ball?

can   I _____ throw it.

get   Will he _____ it?

will   Yes, he _____.

got   Have you _____ a cat?

her   What is _____ name?

my   This is _____ dad.

is   His name _____ Bob.

go   We must _____ home.

it   What time is _____?

in   Can I go _____?

but   Yes, _____ be quick!

had   Have you _____ lunch?

not   No, I have _____!

went   We _____ on the bus.

from   Where _____?

the   I want to get _____ train back.

and   Yes, _____ get food!

Make up your own sentence with one or more of these words.

_____

_____.

Two letters, one sound

Some sounds are made up of more than one letter, like "ck."
This is called a digraph. Here are four more digraphs.
Say the words out loud to hear the "ch," "sh," "th," and "ng" sounds.

<u>ch</u>ick   <u>sh</u>ip   <u>th</u>umb   ri<u>ng</u>

Word wizard

Help the wizard make words by writing in "ch," "sh," "th," or "ng."
Read the words out loud.

ba_ _   ba_ _   ba_ _   wi_ _

ri_ _   wi_ _

_ _in

ri_ _   _ _in   _ _in

Pirate puzzle

Only one of these chests contains the treasure map.
It is the one without a real word on the front. Which one is it?

Pirate adventure

Fill in the blanks using some of the words from above. Don't forget to use a capital letter!

_____ pirates know _____ is treasure under a palm

tree, but is it _____ tree or _____ tree?

Vowel sounds

Vowel sounds can also be made up of two letters. Say these words out loud to hear the "oa," "ee," "oo," and "ea" sounds.

boat   **tree**   **book**   **spoon**   **bean**   **bread**

Alien abduction

These aliens need vowel sounds to power their ships. Find the vowel sounds in the words below and write the two letters that make them on the spaceships.

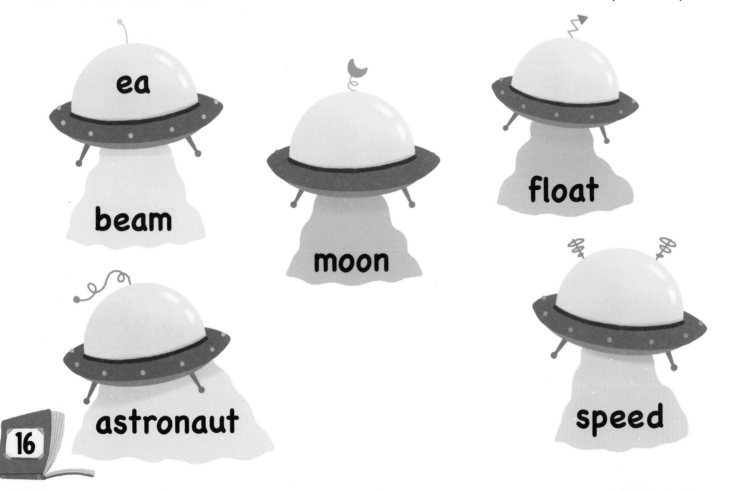

ea

beam

moon

float

astronaut

speed

16

Follow the trails

These animals can only go through words with the same vowel sounds.
Draw their paths to find out where they are going.

snail	kangaroo	goat	sheep
tail	too	coat	sleep
zoo	fail	seen	oak
food	queen	brain	toast
green	shoo	soap	again
greed	toad	boo	rain
weed	soon	road	stain

 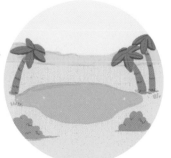  

Vowels with r

Say these words out loud to hear the "ar," "or," "er," "ir," and "ur" sounds. Notice that "er," "ir," and "ur" make the same sound, but the spellings are different.

 star
 door
 mermaid
 bird
 turtle

Animal magic

Underline the correct spelling for each of the animals shown below.

caterpillar
caterpiller

tertle
turtle

bird
burd

kangeroo
kangaroo

gorilla
girilla

Job search

These "vowels with r" sounds are often at the end of words and can be tricky to choose the right spelling. Read these words and find them in the grid.

teacher   sister   actor   painter   author   doctor

b	a	e	r	o	s	m	q	z	c
f	d	r	p	a	i	n	t	e	r
q	t	d	l	v	s	r	e	x	t
w	y	o	p	m	t	w	a	d	f
c	u	c	o	k	e	r	c	s	a
a	u	t	h	o	r	y	h	o	n
a	b	o	e	r	j	r	e	s	m
k	b	r	a	c	t	o	r	g	s

Blended sounds

Some consonants are often together in words. They make a blended sound.
In the word "frog," the "f" and "r" blend to make "fr."

f + r = _fr_og

This is not a digraph because the letters make two different sounds,
but they are blended into one spelling sound.

Beach blends

Look at each picture and say what you see.
Listen for the beginning blend and write in the missing letters.

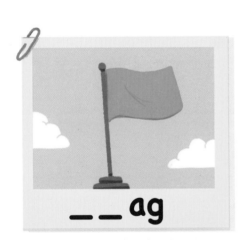

_ _ ag

_ _ im

_ _ ab

_ _ asses

_ _ ane

_ _ ink

Something fishy

Nine of these fish have letter blends that go together.
One has letters that don't blend. Which one?

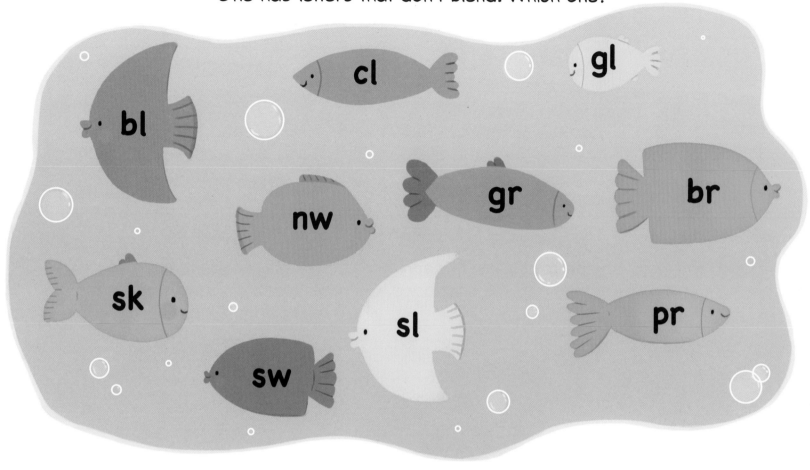

Building blends

On the yellow bricks are blends that you might hear at the end of words.
How many words can you make by putting the yellow bricks with the green bricks?

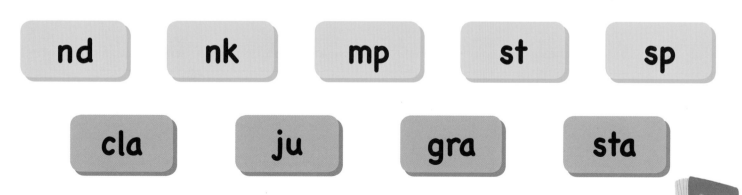

Segmenting

Segmenting is hearing all the sounds that make up a word.
It is the opposite of blending, but it is important for spelling.

b r i ck

The word "brick" has five letters but four sounds. The "b" and the "r" combine into a blended sound. The "ck" is a digraph, where two letters make one sound.

Trundling trains

Read the words below and listen to each sound. Follow the example above and write the sounds into the carriages, with one sound on each part.

track   ticket   steam

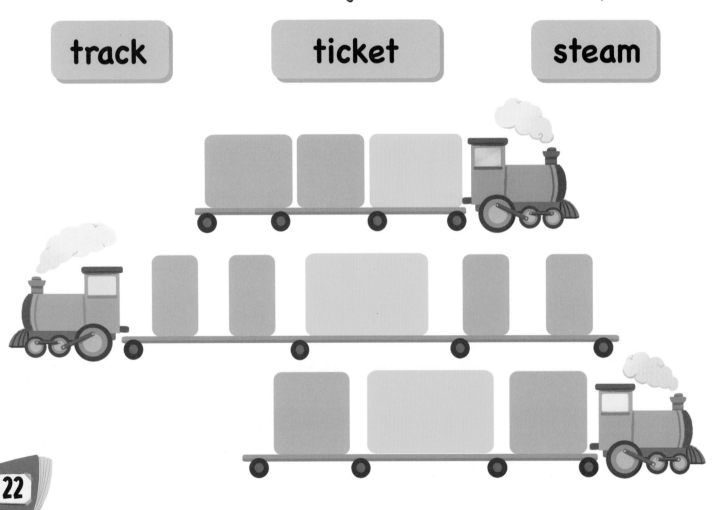

Robot talk

This talking robot repeats words but separates each sound.
Fill in the missing sounds, for the words that follow the example.

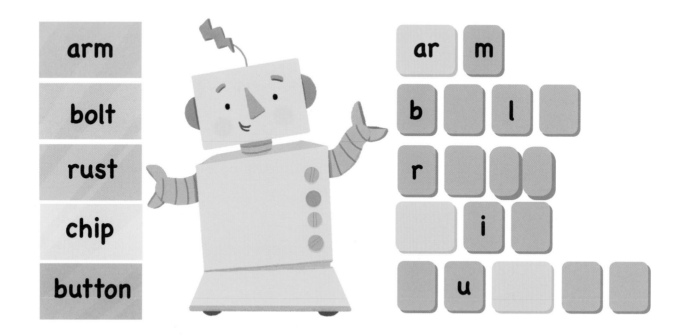

arm

bolt

rust

chip

button

ar m

b   l

r

i

u

Jungle jumble

The sounds in these jungle words have been jumbled up.
Can you put them back in the right order?

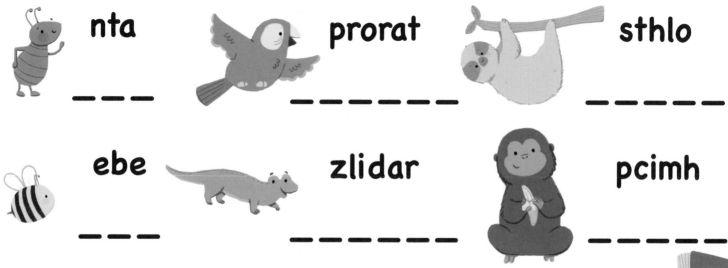

nta

_ _ _

prorat

_ _ _ _ _ _

sthlo

_ _ _ _ _

ebe

_ _ _

zlidar

_ _ _ _ _ _

pcimh

_ _ _ _ _

Syllables

Long words can be split into beats, called syllables, to help you spell them. Each syllable has a vowel. For example, these words each have three syllables:

kangaroo = kang-a-roo

chimpanzee = chim-pan-zee

Broken down this way, really long words become easier to spell, and even easier to read.

School days

Here are some school words, broken into syllables.
Note the beats as you write each word by its picture.

class-room   pen-cil   chil-dren   teach-er   sharp-en-er

Dinosaur days

Here are some things that dinosaurs love to do. Write "ing" at the end of each word below, and read them out loud. Can you hear the two syllables?

play_ _ _

snor_ _ _

sleep_ _ _

roar_ _ _

runn_ _ _

fight_ _ _

Days of the week

Here are the days of the week. How many syllables does each day have?
Write the numbers in the boxes.

Monday

Tuesday

Wednesday

Thursday

Friday

Saturday

Sunday

Sight words

Here are more sight words to learn. Read each one,
say it out loud, cover it up, and then write it in the sentence.

that   What is _____?

you   I can't tell _____.

me   You can tell _____.

was   It _____ my school book.

by   It was bitten _____ my dog.

children   Does he bite _____?

no   _____!

just   _____ school books.

help   I can _____.

fix   We can _____ it.

at	Look _____ that!
good	It looks _____.
as	Good _____ new.
are	You _____ kind.
into	Put it _____ the bag.
so	I am _____ happy.
on	Come _____.
to	Where _____?
for	We can go _____ ice cream.
all	With _____ the toppings!

Make up your own sentence with one or more of these words.

_____

_____.

Three letters, one sound

Sometimes a sound is made up of three letters. This is called a trigraph.
Say these words out loud to hear the "igh," "ear," "air," and "ure" sounds.

night   ear   chair   picture

Word wizard

Help the wizard make real words by adding the endings "igh," "ear," "air," and "ure." Be careful! Not all letter and ending combinations will make real words.

h_ _ _

s_ _ _

s_ _ _

f_ _ _

h_ _ _

f_ _ _

p_ _ _

h_ _ _

p_ _ _

p_ _ _

Trundling trolleys

Read the words below and listen to each sound.
Write the sounds into the carriages, with one sound on each part.

| stair | tight | capture |

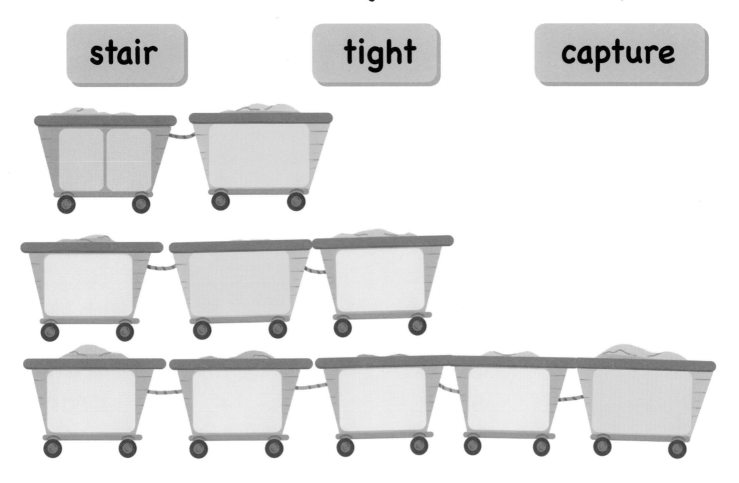

Peter Pan

Underline the only word that has three syllables (beats).

adventure
moonlight
fearless
fairy

The ai sound

When you hear the "ai" sound in a word, it can be spelled in lots of ways.
Here are the three most common:

ai as in tr<u>ai</u>n   ay as in d<u>ay</u>   a_e as in f<u>ade</u>

The spelling "ay" is often at the end of words.

Picture match

Underline the correct spelling.

snale
snail
snayl

crane
crain
crayn

cake
caik
cayk

tale
tail
tayl

mane
main
mayn

It's my birthday

Write the following words into the invitation in the correct order.

Sanjay   **play**   **Friday**   **birthday**   **games**

Dear _____

It's my _____ on _____.

Can you come to ____ _____?

Rhyming words

Copy the spelling patterns to write the rhyming words.

flame bl___   s___   n___

cave w___   br___   g___

nail h___   s___   m___

This creature doesn't follow the "ai" spelling pattern.
Write the correct spelling here:

w h___

31

The oi sound

When you hear the "oi" sound in a word, it can be spelled in two ways.

oy as in t<u>oy</u>   oi as in c<u>oi</u>n

The spelling "oy" is often at the end of words.

"Oi" words

Complete these "oi" words.

s _ _ l

_ _ l

c _ _ n

b _ _ l

p _ _ nt

v _ _ ce

_ _ nk!

Quiz master

Read the clues and then write the correct "oy" word in each of the spaces.

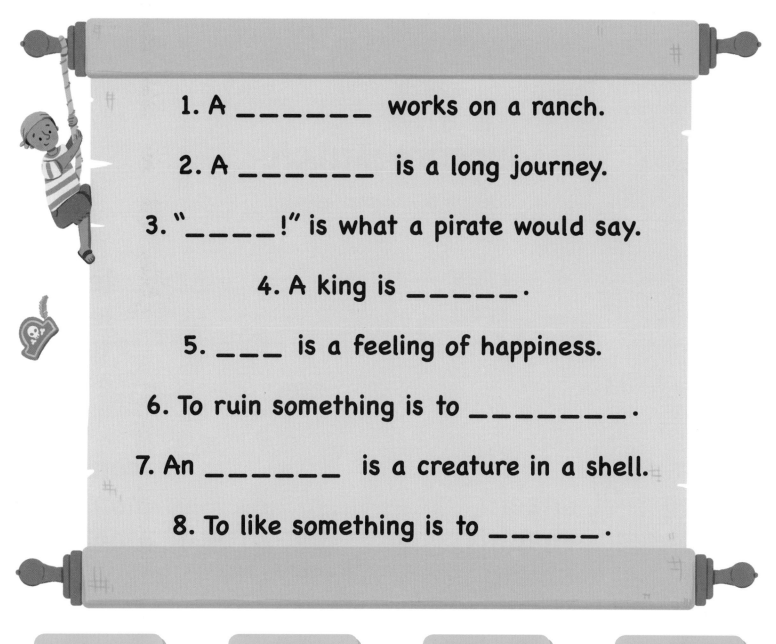

1. A _____ works on a ranch.

2. A _____ is a long journey.

3. "_____!" is what a pirate would say.

4. A king is _____.

5. ____ is a feeling of happiness.

6. To ruin something is to _____.

7. An _____ is a creature in a shell.

8. To like something is to _____.

oyster   Ahoy   destroy   enjoy

cowboy   Joy   voyage   royal

The long e sound

The "long e" sound is spelled in lots of ways. Here are the most common:

ee as in s<u>ee</u>   ea as in p<u>ea</u>   ey as in k<u>ey</u>   e_e as in th<u>eme</u>

ie as in th<u>ie</u>f   e as in <u>e</u>mu   y as in happ<u>y</u>

Picture match

Underline the correct spelling.

tree
trea
trie

leef
leaf
lief

sheeld
sheald
shield

monkee
monkea
monkey

been
bean
bien

coffee
coffea
coffy

Bees love honey

Read the words in this honeycomb. They all have the "long e" sound, but which five words are spelled incorrectly?

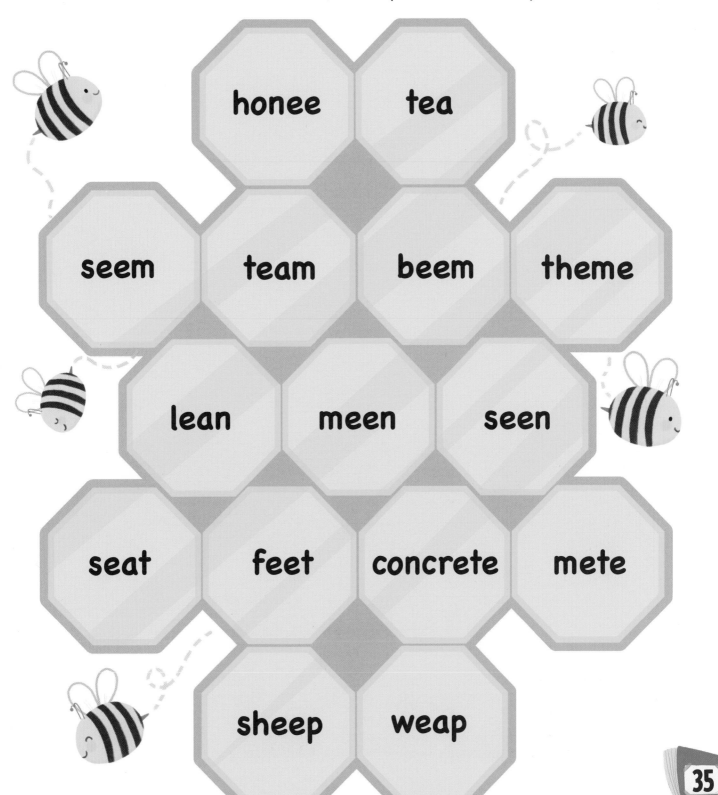

honee

tea

seem

team

beem

theme

lean

meen

seen

seat

feet

concrete

mete

sheep

weap

"i" before "e"

Have you heard the rule "'i' before "e" except after "c?"' It is not always the case! Decide whether you should write "ie" or "ei" into each of these words. There are two "ei" words.

f_ _ld

c_ _ling

w_ _rd

fr_ _nd

Tricky words

Which one of these "long e" words is not a real word?

he	she	ve	me	we	be

Superheroes

Choose a word from this list to make up these superheroes' names.

Speedy Fiery Flappy Stretchy Friendly

_____ Rocket

_____ Girl

Super _____

_____ Avenger

_____ Lightning

The igh sound

The "igh" sound is spelled in different ways, too. Here are the most common:

ie as in t<u>ie</u>   igh as in s<u>igh</u>   y as in b<u>y</u>   i_e as in b<u>i</u>k<u>e</u>

Trundling tractors

Read the words below and listen to each sound.
Write the sounds into the trailers, with one sound on each part.

lie   thigh   fight   fright

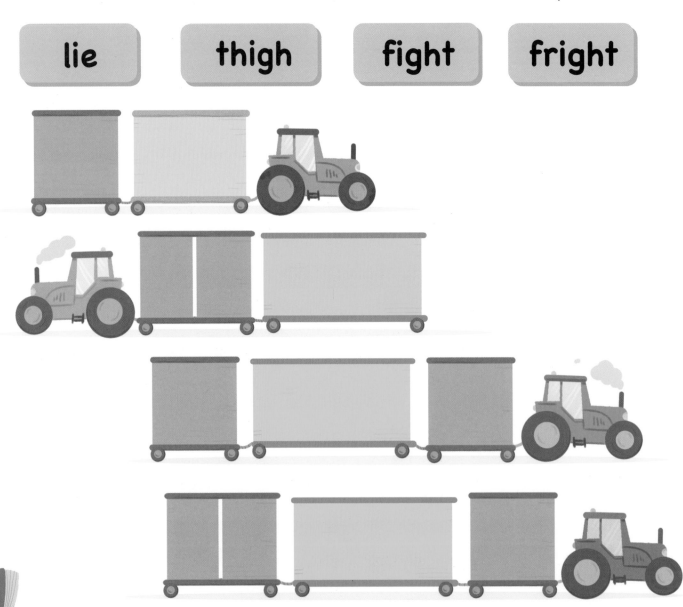

Rhyming words

Write the rhyming word that goes with each of the pictures below.

sky _ _ _

tie _ _ _

right _ _ _ _ _ _

dried _ _ _ _ _

Tricky words

These two words do not follow the pattern. Write them in the sentences.

height   eight

My twin is my _ _ _ _ _ _ _.

We are _ _ _ _ _ years old.

The ou sound

When you hear the "ou" sound in a word, it can be spelled in two ways:

ow as in <u>now</u>   ou as in sh<u>out</u>

The spelling "ow" is often at the end of words.

Rhyming words

Copy the spelling patterns to write the rhyming words.

cow b__ w__ h__ n__

clown d___ br___ dr___ t___

Can you write a sentence about a brown cow meeting a clown?

_____.

40

A crowd of clouds

This helicopter can only go through clouds with "ou" words.
Can you find a way down to the helipad?

flower

ground

allow

crown

out

bow

spout

power

frown

sound

owl

brow

The oa sound

The "oa" sound is spelled in different ways, too. Here are the most common:

oa as in <u>oa</u>k   ow as in gr<u>ow</u>   oe as in t<u>oe</u>

o_e as in h<u>o</u>p<u>e</u>   o as in hell<u>o</u>

Let it snow

Read the words on the snowman's belly. How many of each spelling are there?
Write the numbers on the snowflakes.

ow
___

oe
___

oa
___

snow   blow

toe   nose   float

slope   foe   own

coat   toad

o_e
___

42

Pick a letter

Using these six letters, can you spell the words to match the pictures below?

o   a   l   p   n   e   w

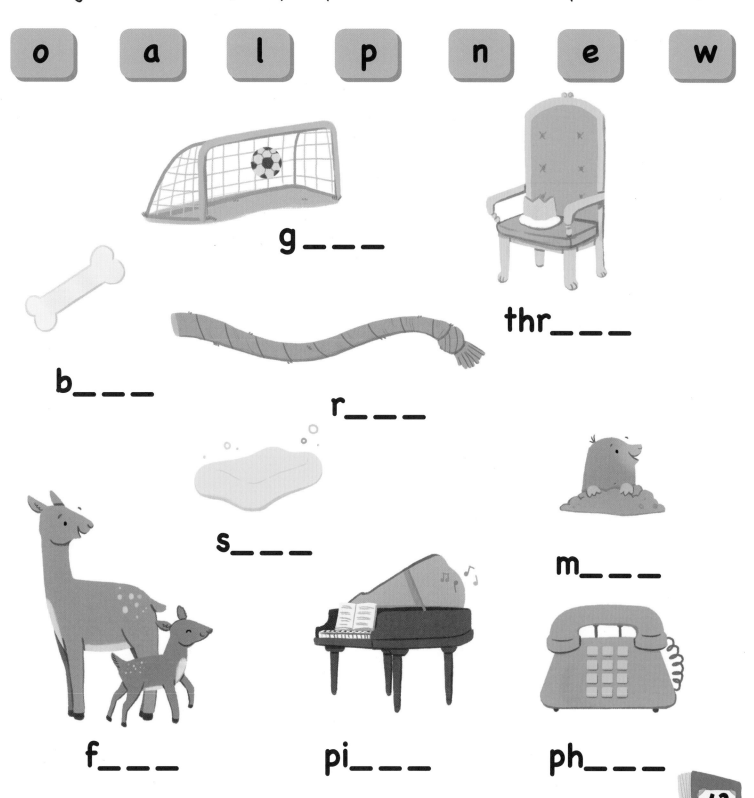

g _ _ _

thr _ _ _

b _ _ _

r _ _ _

s _ _ _

m _ _ _

f _ _ _

pi _ _ _

ph _ _ _

The yoo sound

The "yoo" sound is spelled in different ways, too. Here are the most common:

u_e as in <u>June</u>   oo as in f<u>oo</u>d   ue as in bl<u>ue</u>   ew as in fl<u>ew</u>

Picture match

Underline the correct spelling.

ruler
rooler
rewler

floot
flewt
flute

gloo
glew
glue

scewter
scuter
scooter

cube
cueb
cewb

Rhyming words

Copy the spelling patterns to write the rhyming words.

blue   cl_ _ tr_ _   arg_ _
blew   fl_ _ thr_ _ n_ _

Can you write a sentence about a blue balloon that blew away?

_____.

Me too!

These three words all sound the same but mean different things.
Write them in the correct places in the sentence below.

too   two   to

The _ _ _ children went _ _ the store

and their goose came, _ _ _ !

"Two" is the number 2.
"Too" means <u>also</u> or <u>very</u>.

The er sound

The "er" sound has three spellings:

ir as in s<u>ir</u>   ur as in f<u>ur</u>   er as in h<u>er</u>

T-shirts

Look at the pictures on the T-shirts. How do you spell the word,
with an "ir," "ur," or "er?" Use the correct crayon to brighten them up.

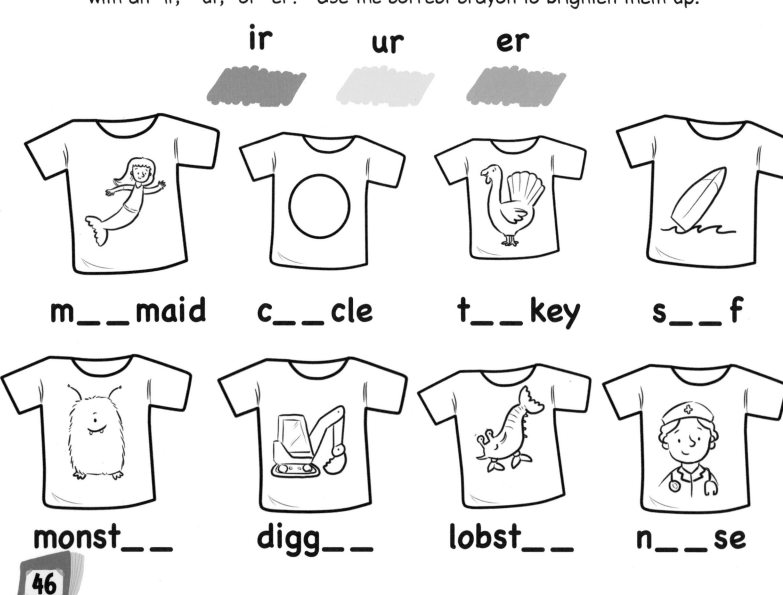

ir

ur

er

m_ _ _maid   c_ _ _cle   t_ _ key   s_ _ _f

monst_ _   digg_ _   lobst_ _   n_ _ _se

Finish the sentences

Complete these sentences by using "ir," "ur," and "er" in the correct places.

The b_ _ d was on its p_ _ ch.

The tig_ _ has stripy f_ _ .

The t_ _ tle was in the wat_ _ .

The s_ _ f_ _ came f_ _ st.

The g_ _ l wore a sk_ _ t.

The or sound

The "or" sound is spelled in different ways, too. Here are the most common:

aw as in s<u>aw</u>   au as in <u>au</u>thor   or as in f<u>or</u>

ore as in m<u>ore</u>   oor as in d<u>oor</u>

Trundling trains

Read the words and listen to each sound. Write the words into the trains, with one sound on each part.

August   poor   shore   straw

Picture match

Underline the correct spelling.

astronawt
astronort
astronaut

prawn
prorn
praun

caw
core
coor

dore
daur
door

hawse
horse
hoors

Rhyming words

Read this sentence, cover it up, and then write it below.

I saw a fawn being born in an August storm.

_____.

The ear sound

When you hear the "ear" sound in a word, it can be spelled in two ways.

ear as in f<u>ear</u>   eer as in ch<u>eer</u>

Rhyming words

Copy the spelling patterns to write the rhyming words.

hear   g_ _ _   d_ _ _   r_ _ _   f_ _ _

cheer   sh_ _ _   d_ _ _   sn_ _ _   st_ _ _

Tricky words

Some words sound the same but have different spellings and meanings.
Complete the sentences below using the correct spellings.

| deer | dear | hear | here |

I can h_ _ _ a d_ _ _.

H_ _ _ is my d_ _ _ grandma.

Quiz master

Read the clues and then write the correct "ear" word in each of the spaces.

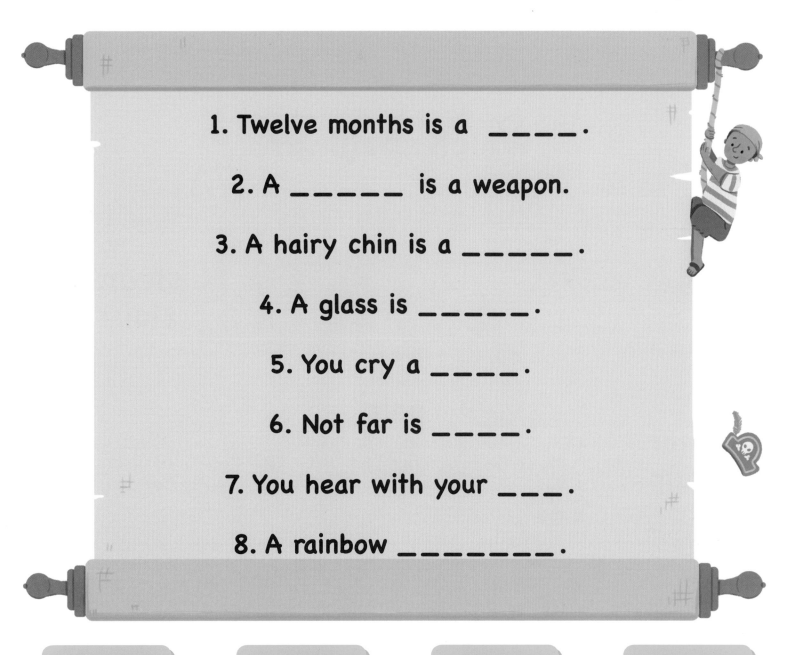

1. Twelve months is a _ _ _ _ _ .

2. A _ _ _ _ _ _ is a weapon.

3. A hairy chin is a _ _ _ _ _ _ .

4. A glass is _ _ _ _ _ _ .

5. You cry a _ _ _ _ _ .

6. Not far is _ _ _ _ _ .

7. You hear with your _ _ _ _ .

8. A rainbow _ _ _ _ _ _ _ _ .

beard   spear   tear   clear

ear   near   appears   year

The air sound

When you hear the "air" sound in a word, it is usually spelled in one of three ways.

air as in h<u>air</u>   ear as in w<u>ear</u>   are as in c<u>are</u>

Which spelling?

The spellings "ear" and "air" can sometimes sound the same.
Underline the correct spelling.

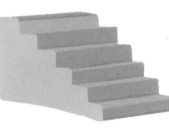

stears
stairs

pear
pair

tear
tair

pear
pair

fairground
fareground

hare
hair

Goldilocks

Read this story and listen for the "air" sound in the words. Underline them when you find them. There is also an "air" word spelled "eir." Can you find it?

For a dare, Goldilocks, who has long blonde hair, went to the house of the three bears. She sat in their chairs, ate their porridge, and then went upstairs to bed.

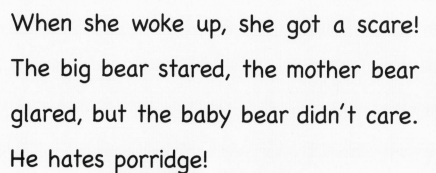

When she woke up, she got a scare! The big bear stared, the mother bear glared, but the baby bear didn't care. He hates porridge!

The ph sound

There is an alternative spelling for the "f" sound:

ph as in p̲honics

Some words we use a lot have the "f" sound with a "ph" spelling.

Correct the spelling

Correct the spellings of these words.

dolfin

_ _ _ _ _ _ _

foto

_ _ _ _ _

alfabet

_ _ _ _ _ _ _ _

fone

_ _ _ _ _

elefant

_ _ _ _ _ _ _ _

nefew

_ _ _ _ _

The j sound

When you hear the "j" sound at the end of a word, it is spelled in one of two ways:

ge as in hu<u>ge</u>   dge as in he<u>dge</u>

The letter "g" sometimes makes a soft sound, as in "giraffe."

Jack and the giant

Underline nine words with the letter "g" that have a soft "j" sound.

Jack lived in a cottage in the village.
He met a strange man who gave him
magic beans, which grew into
a gigantic beanstalk!

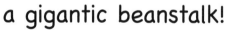

Jack climbed up and found a huge
castle. It was home to a giant who
was taller than a giraffe! Jack was
in danger!

The soft c

Read the word "circus." The first "c" makes the same sound as "s" in "six." This is called a "soft c," and it is usually followed by "e," "i," or "y."

Word scramble

Use the picture clues to unscramble the "soft c" words.

iecd   ciem   bceciyl

_ _ _ _   _ _ _ _   _ _ _ _ _ _ _

Syllable stitch up

Here are six syllables. Using the picture clues, can you put them together to make three "soft c" words?

cir   cess   cil   pen   cle   prin

_ _ _ _ _ _   _ _ _ _ _ _   _ _ _ _ _ _ _

Hidden picture

Shade only the sections of this picture that contain words with the "soft c" sound to reveal a hidden picture.

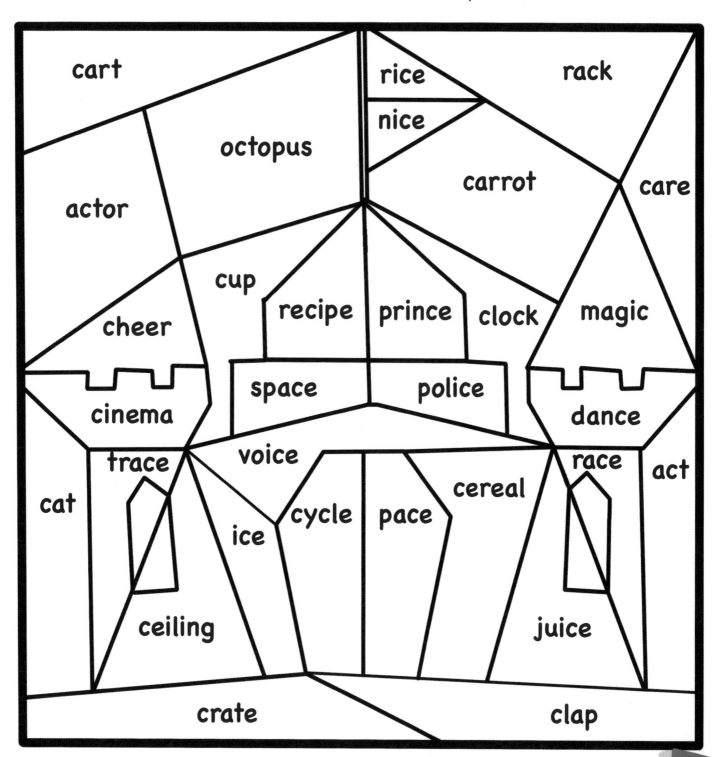

cart

rice

rack

nice

octopus

carrot

care

actor

cup

cheer

recipe

prince

clock

magic

space

police

dance

cinema

trace

voice

race

act

cat

cycle

pace

cereal

ice

ceiling

juice

crate

clap

Silent letters

Some letters hide in words, so you can't hear them. They make spelling very hard! The best at hiding are these six letters:

t h b k w g

Hide and seek

Say these words out loud and then underline the silent letter.

 hutch    gnome    school

 thumb    knife    wreck

Correct the spelling

Four spellings are incorrect in this sentence. Write the sentence correctly below.

This is the night hoo lives in a wite casle.

_____

_____ .

The gnome's garden

Separate these words into their silent letter groups. One has been done for you.

sign   match   sword

where   hour   design   ~~lamb~~

know   comb   listen   climb

ghost   knee   write   knot

silent b

lamb

silent k

silent w

silent h

silent t

silent g

Syllable practice

You have learned to spell a lot of words! Now, with gorilla as an example, write down the animal names and put the number of syllables for each word in the boxes.

gorilla   3

k_____

d_____

s_____

r_____

l___

e_____

Months of the year

With January as an example, write down each of the months, and then put the number of syllables for each word in the boxes.

Be careful! One month has a silent letter!

01	January	4
02	F_____	
03	M_____	
04	A_____	
05	M__	
06	J___	
07	J___	
08	A_____	
09	S_____	
10	O_____	
11	N_____	
12	D_____	

Plurals

A plural is more than one. Plurals end with "s" or "es."

one truck   two truck<u>s</u>

one bus   two bus<u>es</u>

You add "es" when the word ends with "o," "s," "sh," "ch," "x," "z."

The farmers' market

Help the farmer by finishing the words on his signs, as shown.

carrot<u>s</u>

melon___

banana___

peach___

pear___

apple___

tomato___

62

Watch out for "y!"

When a word ends in "y," its plural can sometimes be "ies," often if the letter before is a consonant. Follow the examples to find the plurals of these words.

1 boy
2 boys

1 baby
2 babies

1 toy
2 toy _

1 story
2 stor_ _ _

1 key
2 key _

1 penny
2 penn_ _ _

Puzzling plurals

Below are the plurals of some common words that have no rule.
Underline the correct spellings.

thief	thiefs thieves	man	mans men
sheep	sheeps sheep	tooth	tooths teeth
child	childs children	mouse	mouses mice

Verb endings

Verbs are action words. You add "s" or "es" to action words when describing what someone else is doing.

I grow.   A plant grow<u>s</u>.   I watch.   My dad watch<u>es</u>.

It is "es" when the word ends with "o," "s," "sh," "ch," "x," "z."

Bear's playground

What does Bear do? Finish the words.

Bear climb<u>s</u>   **Bear play__**   **Bear catch__**

Bear splash__   **Bear fix__**   **Bear draw__**

Watch out for "y!"

When an action word ends with a consonant + "y," the ending changes to "ies." Follow the examples and write in the other correct endings.

I cry.
My sister cr<u>ies</u>.

I play.
My brother pl<u>ays</u>.

I hurry.
Joshua hurr_ _ _.

I enjoy it.
Dad enjo_ _ it.

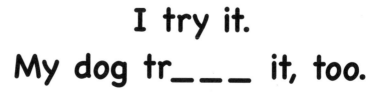

I try it.
My dog tr_ _ _ it, too.

Adding ed and ing

Action words (verbs) change depending on when the action happened.

I walk   I am walk<u>ing</u>   I walk<u>ed</u>

If the word ends with "e," you drop the "e" to add "ing" or "ed."

I wav<u>e</u> I am wav<u>ing</u> I wav<u>ed</u>

Monkey mayhem

Add "ing" to these action words. Don't forget to drop the "e" if there is one.

kick **<u>kicking</u>**   throw _____   catch _____

make _____   count _____   hide _____

Magic spells

This wizard has got into a muddle making "ing" and "ed" words. Can you spot three spelling mistakes? What should they be (one doesn't follow a rule at all!)?

mixing

wishing

bakeing

gived

hopeing

baked

wished

giving

hoped

floated

floating

Y verbs

When an action word ends with a vowel + "y," you add "ing" and "ed" to the word. If the word ends with a consonant + "y," you drop the "y" and add "ied." Complete these columns following the examples.

	<u>ing</u>	<u>(i)ed</u>
play	play<u>ing</u>	play<u>ed</u>
cry	cry<u>ing</u>	cr<u>ied</u>
dry		
study		
enjoy		
carry		

Double up!

When an action word has only one syllable and ends with a vowel + a consonant, the last consonant is doubled. Copy the example.

I shop   I am shopping   I shopped

I hop   I am hop_ _ _ _   I hop_ _ _

Playful penguins

What are the penguins doing? Add "ing" to these action words.
Don't forget to double up the last consonant.

stop_ _ _ _ _   skid_ _ _ _ _   run_ _ _ _ _

flap_ _ _ _ _   plod_ _ _ _ _   hug_ _ _ _ _

Now, write what each penguin <u>did</u>, by adding "ed." Be careful.
There is no such word as "runned." Write the correct word instead.

stop_ _ _   skid_ _ _   r_ _

flap_ _ _   plod_ _ _   hug_ _ _

Sight words

Have you remembered these sight words? Read each one, say it out loud, cover it up, and then write it in the sentence.

the   What is _____ time?

a   Time to do _____ handstand!

are   You _____ funny!

do   How did you ____ that?

today   I learned to swim _____.

said   "Clever!" _____ Dad.

says   "Thanks," _____ the boy.

What is the girl asking the boy?
Choose three words and write them in.

you   be   he   me   she   we

"When will ____ ____ the same age as _____?"

Look at these words. Two are not real words.
Which two? Write the correct spellings below.

was

were

has

is

thay

no

his

come

go

so

luve

of

my

house

put

friend

by

school

pull

once

The correct spellings are:

_____   _____

Tricky words

Words that sound the same but have different meanings or spellings are called homophones.

pear   pair

Pear pairs

Can you find the matching pairs?

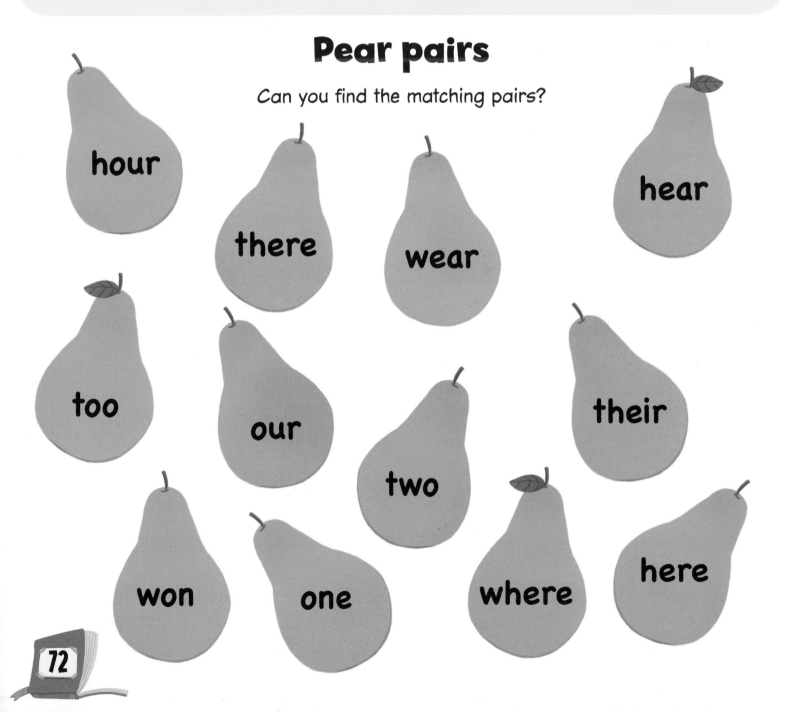

hour

there

wear

hear

too

our

two

their

won

one

where

here

72

Night knight

Look at these pictures. Write the correct spelling underneath each image.

see sea	bear bare	night knight
hair hare	eight ate	write right

_ _ _   _ _ _   _ _ _ _   _ _ _ _

_ _ _ _ _   _ _ _ _ _   _ _ _ _   _ _ _ _

_ _ _ _ _   _ _ _ _ _   _ _ _ _   _ _ _

Joining words

Two words can join together to make one word.

foot + ball = football   bed + room = bedroom

Break down these words to make them easier to spell.

Jigsaw puzzle

Look at the dominoes. What whole words are they making?

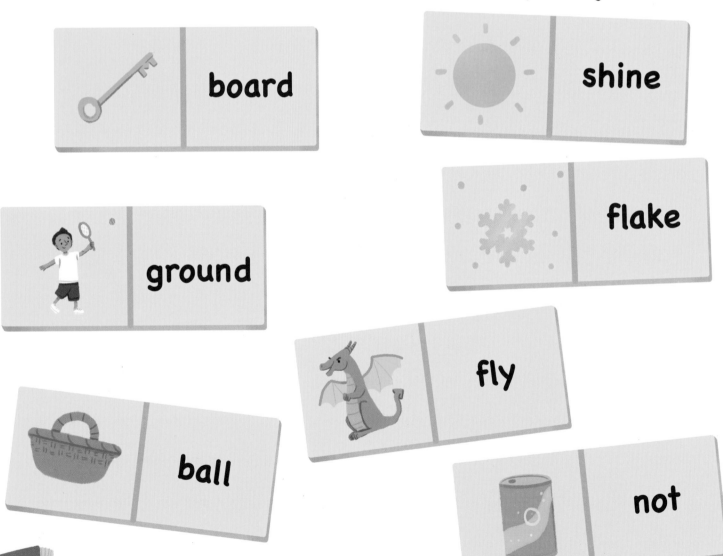

board

shine

ground

flake

fly

ball

not

Word builder

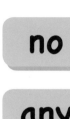

How many whole words can you make from these words?

no	where	some	time
any	thing	every	way

What's the word?

Can you guess the words these picture pairs are making?

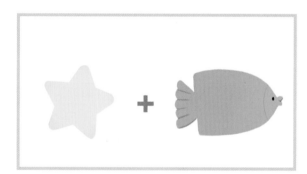

The ul sound

Listen out for the "ul" sound at the end of words. It is tricky to know what the spelling should be. The most common endings are:

le as in cast<u>le</u>   al as in ped<u>al</u>   el as in tunn<u>el</u>   il as in penc<u>il</u>

Pick a spelling

Underline the correct spelling.

apple
appal

animle
animal

corle
coral

bottle
bottal

hospitel hospital

cerele
cereal

middle
middal

tunnel
tunnle

littel
little

Follow the trails

These animals can only go through words with the same "ul" sound spelling.
Draw their paths to find out where they are going.

gerbil	eagle	jackal	squirrel
pencil	tickle	petal	parcel
stencil	capital	double	barrel
nostril	puddle	vocal	chapel
gentle	April	angel	musical
evil	beetle	magical	jewel
fossil	plural	table	travel

Endings that sound like shun

When you hear the sound "shun" at the end of words, it is often spelled "tion," but there are other spellings. The most common are:

tion as in st<u>a</u>t<u>ion</u>   **sion** as in vi<u>sion</u>

Attention!

Complete these words with "tion" and read them out loud.

na_____

fic_____

ac_____

subtrac_____

frac_____

sec_____

peti_____

addi_____

Complete the sentences

Write these words into the sentences.

station | television | mansion | potion | portion

The train stopped

at the _ _ _ _ _ _ _.

I love watching _ _ _ _ _ _ _ _ _ _ _.

The family lived in a _ _ _ _ _ _ _ _.

The wizard made a _ _ _ _ _ _ _.

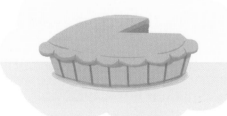

Do you want a

_ _ _ _ _ _ _ _ of pie?

Suffixes

Suffixes are letter groups that are added to the end of words to make different words. Here are some of the most common:

ful   less   ly   ment   ness

Clumsy clown

Is the clown being careful or careless? Write the correct word underneath.

care____   care_____   care____   care_____

Suffix puzzle

Choose a suffix to make a new word. There may be more than one choice.

ful   ness   ly   ment   less

help_____   enjoy_____   slow___

sad_____   tear____   pain____

80

How do they do it?

Add the describing word you think fits the animal best. There are several answers.

excitedly   strangely   quickly

bravely   expertly   happily

Fox runs _____.

Penguin skates _____.

Rabbit hops _____.

Dog eats _____.

Duck swims _____.

Crocodile dances _____.

More suffixes

Here are two more suffixes that can be added to describing words:

er   est

When a word ends with "y," you drop the "y" and add "ier" and "iest."

Word whales

Add "er" and "est" to these words, and read them out loud.

cold
cold_ _
cold_ _ _

kind
kind_ _
kind_ _ _

Drop the "e".

wise
wis_ _
wis_ _ _

nice
nic_ _
nic_ _ _

Drop the "y" and add "i".

silly
sill_ _ _
sill_ _ _ _

happy
happ_ _ _
happ_ _ _ _

82

Dinosaur families

Write the words underneath the pictures, following the examples. When a describing word has only one syllable and ends with a vowel + a consonant, double up!

heavy   heavier   heaviest

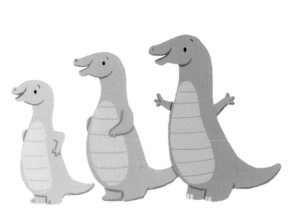

big   bigger   biggest

fast   fast_ _   fast_ _ _

fat   fat_ _ _   fat_ _ _ _

cute   cut_ _   cut_ _ _

scary   scar_ _ _   scar_ _ _ _

It is, it's not!

Some words we use are two words put together and shortened, for example "it is" becomes "it's." The apostrophe shows that letters are missing. These words are called contractions.

I will becomes I'll   did not becomes didn't

Sausage dogs

Following the example, write each set of two words as one word on the puppies. Put the apostrophe where the letter is missing.

you are

you're

is not

I am

let us

Contrary Mary

Contrary Mary disagrees with everyone! Follow the example and write her responses in the speech bubbles.

Look, say, cover, write

Look at the words. Say them out loud. Cover them up.
Write them. Check the word and try again if you get it wrong.

Look and say	Cover and write	Check and write again
door		
floor		
because		
find		
kind		
behind		
child		
children		
wild		
climb		
most		
only		

Look and say	Cover and write	Check and write again
both		
old		
cold		
told		
every		
everybody		
even		
great		
pretty		
dog		
after		
fast		

Look, say, cover, write

Look at the words. Say them out loud. Cover them up.
Write them. Try again if you get it wrong.

Look and say	Cover and write	Check and write again
last		
father		
mother		
class		
grass		
bath		
move		
sure		
sugar		
would		
could		
should		

Look and say	Cover and write	Check and write again
eye		
who		
whole		
many		
clothes		
busy		
people		
water		
again		
money		
half		
parents		

Solutions

Page 4 Alphabet bricks

a b c d e
f g h i j
k l m n o
p q r s t
u v w x y z

Page 5 Picture crossword

	b					d		
h	e	n			f	o	x	
	d			c		g		
		y	a	k				
	l			t		r		
p	i	g			b	u	n	
	p					g		

Page 5 By the sea

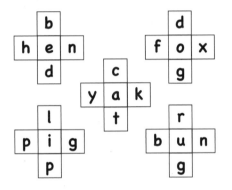

fish   ship   crab   ball   sun

Page 6 The word a

A dog and <u>a</u> cat lived in <u>a</u> house on <u>a</u> hill.

Page 7 What is that?

<u>an</u> eye   <u>an</u> ear
<u>a</u> nose   <u>a</u> cheek
<u>a</u> mouth

Page 7 The word I

When <u>I</u> walk down the street,
<u>I</u> never think about my feet.
<u>I</u> sometimes wonder how they know
where it is <u>I</u> want to go.

Page 8 The king's castle

krown
crown
cing
king
kloak
cloak
kar
car
castle
kastle

Page 9 Watch out!

<u>wasp</u>   <u>wand</u>   <u>worm</u>
<u>watch</u>   <u>world</u>

Page 9 Tricky, tricky

When I was one, I learned to run.

When I was two, I went to the zoo.

When I was three, I learned ABC.

When I was four, I learned lots more!

Page 10 Duck's truck

Here is Duck in his <u>pik-up</u> truck.

The truck is <u>stuk</u> in mud and <u>muk</u>.

They don't have much <u>luc</u>,

Duck and his truck.

pick-up stuck muck luck

Page 11 Double letters

cliff, well, all/ass, off, buzz/ bull/buff, dress, kiss/kill

Page 11 Tricky words

I will push <u>if</u> you pull.
Look at <u>us</u>!
The boy missed the <u>bus</u>.
Do cows give us milk? <u>Yes</u>!

Page 14 Word wizard
Any of these:
rich, ring, bath, bash, bang, wing, wish, chin, shin, thin

Page 15 Pirate puzzle

thay

Page 15 Pirate adventure

<u>The</u> pirates know <u>there</u> is treasure under a palm tree, but is it <u>this</u> tree or <u>that</u> tree?

Page 16 Alien abduction

ea
beam
oo
moon
oa
float
au
astronaut
ee
speed

90

Solutions

Page 17 Follow the trails

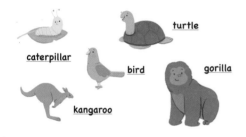

snail	kangaroo	goat	sheep
tail	too	coat	sleep
zoo	fail	seen	oak
food	queen	brain	toast
green	shoo	soap	again
greed	toad	boo	rain
weed	soon	road	stain

Page 18 Animal magic

turtle

caterpillar

bird

gorilla

kangaroo

Page 19 Job search

b	a	e	r	o	s	m	q	z	c
f	d	r	p	a	i	n	t	e	r
q	t	d	l	v	s	r	e	x	t
w	y	o	p	m	t	w	a	d	f
c	u	c	o	k	e	r	c	s	a
a	u	t	h	o	r	y	h	o	n
a	b	o	e	r	j	r	e	s	m
k	b	r	a	c	t	o	r	g	s

Page 20 Beach blends

flag swim crab

glasses plane drink

Page 21 Something fishy

nw

Page 21 Building blends

clank, clamp, clasp, junk, jump, just, grand, grasp, stand, stank, stamp

Page 22 Trundling trains

tr a ck

t i ck e t

st ea m

Page 23 Robot talk

b-o-l-t
r-u-s-t
ch-i-p
b-u-tt-o-n

Page 23 Jungle jumble

ant parrot sloth
bee lizard chimp

Page 24 School days

classroom pencil children teacher sharpener

Page 25 Days of the week

Monday	2	Tuesday	2
Wednesday	2	Thursday	2
Friday	2	Saturday	3
Sunday	2		

Page 25 Dinosaur days

playing sleeping snoring roaring running fighting

Page 28 Word wizard

Any of these:

high, hear, hair, sigh, sure, fear, fair, pear, pair, pure

Page 29 Trundling trolleys

s t air

t igh t

c a p t ure

Page 29 Peter Pan

ad-ven-ture

Page 30 Picture match

snail crane

cake tail mane

91

Solutions

Page 31 It's my birthday

Dear <u>Sanjay</u>
It's my <u>birthday</u> on <u>Friday</u>.
Can you come to <u>play</u> <u>games</u>?

Page 31 Rhyming words

flame, blame, same, name,
cave, wave, brave, gave,
nail, hail, sail, mail,
whale

Page 32 "Oi" words

soil, oil, coin, bowl, oink, point,
voice

Page 33 Quiz master

1. A <u>cowboy</u> works on a ranch.
2. A <u>voyage</u> is a long journey.
3. "<u>Ahoy!</u>" is what a pirate
would say.
4. A king is <u>royal</u>.
5. <u>Joy</u> is a feeling
of happiness.
6. To ruin something is
to <u>destroy</u>.
7. An <u>oyster</u> is a creature in
a shell.
8. To like something is
to <u>enjoy</u>.

Page 34 Picture match

tree

monkey

leaf

shield

bean

coffee

Page 35 Bees love honey

honee (honey), beem (beam),
meen (mean), mete (meet),
weap (weep)

Page 36 "i" before "e"

f<u>ie</u>ld, c<u>ei</u>ling, w<u>ei</u>rd, fr<u>ie</u>nd

Page 36 Tricky words

ve is not a real word

Page 37 Superheroes

These are some possible names:
Speedy Girl, Fiery Rocket,
Flappy Avenger, Super Bendy,
Friendly Lightning.

Page 38 Trundling tractors

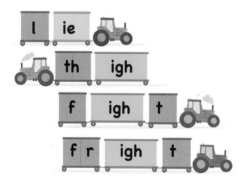

Page 39 Rhyming words

sky, spy; tie, pie; right, light;
dried, cried

Page 39 Tricky words

My twin is my <u>height</u>.
We are <u>eight</u> years old.

Page 40 Rhyming words

cow, bow, wow, how, now,
clown, down, brown, drown,
town

Page 41 A crowd of clouds

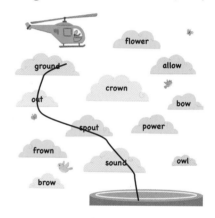

Page 42 Let it snow

ow 3 (snow, blow, own)
oe 2 (toe, foe)
oa 3 (float, coat, toad)
o_e 2 (slope, nose)

Page 43 Pick a letter

goal

throne

bone

rope

soap

mole

fawn

piano

phone

Solutions

Page 44 Picture match

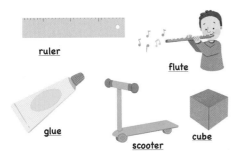

ruler

flute

glue

scooter

cube

Page 45 Rhyming words

blue, clue, true, argue,
blew, flew, threw, new

Page 45 Me too!

The <u>two</u> children went <u>to</u> the
shop and their goose came,
<u>too</u>!

Page 46 T-shirts

mermaid   circle   turkey   surf

monster   digger   lobster   nurse

Page 47 Finish the sentences

The b<u>ir</u>d was on its p<u>er</u>ch.
The tig<u>er</u> has stripy f<u>ur</u>.
The t<u>ur</u>tle was in the wat<u>er</u>.
The s<u>ur</u>f<u>er</u> came f<u>ir</u>st
The g<u>ir</u>l wore a sk<u>ir</u>t.

Page 48 Trundling trains

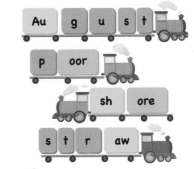

Page 49 Picture match

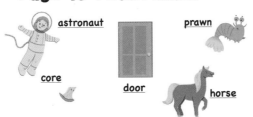

astronaut

prawn

core

door

horse

Page 49 Rhyming words

I saw a fawn being born in
an August storm.

Page 50 Rhyming words

hear, gear, dear, rear, fear,
cheer, sheer, deer, sneer,
steer

Page 50 Tricky words

I can <u>hear</u> a <u>deer</u>.
<u>Here</u> is my <u>dear</u> grandma.

Page 51 Quiz master

1. Twelve months is a <u>year</u>.
2. A <u>spear</u> is a weapon.
3. A hairy chin is a <u>beard</u>.
4. A glass is <u>clear</u>.
5. You cry a <u>tear</u>.
6. Not far is <u>near</u>.
7. You hear with your <u>ear</u>.
8. A rainbow <u>appears</u>.

Page 52 Which spelling?

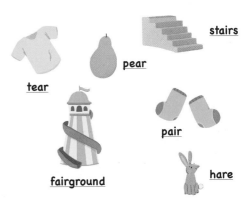

stairs

pear

tear

pair

fairground

hare

Page 53 Goldilocks

Their has an "air" sound.

For a <u>dare</u>, Goldilocks, who has long
blonde <u>hair</u>, went to the house of the
three <u>bears</u>. She sat in <u>their</u> <u>chairs</u>,
ate <u>their</u> porridge, and then went
<u>upstairs</u> to bed.

When she woke up, she got a <u>scare</u>!
The big <u>bear</u> <u>stared</u>, the mother <u>bear</u>
<u>glared</u>, but the baby <u>bear</u> didn't <u>care</u>.
He hates porridge!

The "eir" word is "their."

Page 54 Correct the spelling

dolphin, photo, alphabet,
phone, elephant, nephew

Page 55 Jack and the giant

Jack lived in a <u>cottage</u> in the <u>village</u>.
He met a <u>strange</u> man who gave him
<u>magic</u> beans, which grew into
a <u>gigantic</u> beanstalk!

Jack climbed up and found a <u>huge</u>
castle. It was home to a <u>giant</u> who
was taller than a <u>giraffe</u>! Jack was
in <u>danger</u>!

Page 56 Word scramble

dice mice bicycle

Solutions

Page 56 Syllable stitch up

circle   pencil   princess

Page 57 Hidden picture

Page 58 Hide and seek

hu<u>t</u>ch gnome sc<u>h</u>ool
thum<u>b</u> <u>k</u>nife <u>w</u>reck

Page 58 Correct the spelling

This is the <u>knight</u> <u>who</u> lives in a <u>white</u> <u>castle</u>.

Page 59 The gnome's garden

silent b	silent k
lamb	know
comb	knee
climb	knot

silent w	silent h
sword	where
write	hour
	ghost

silent t	silent g
match	sign
listen	design

Page 60 Syllable practice

kan-ga-roo	3
dol-phin	2
snake	1
rab-bit	2
lion	2
el-e-phant	3

Page 61 Months of the year

02	Feb(r)-u-a-ry	4
03	March	1
04	A-pril	2
05	May	1
06	June	1
07	Ju-ly	2
08	Au-gust	2
09	Sep-tem-ber	3
10	Oc-to-ber	3
11	No-vem-ber	3
12	De-cem-ber	3

Page 62 The farmers' market

carrot<u>s</u>
melon<u>s</u>
banana<u>s</u>
peach<u>es</u>
tomato<u>es</u>
apple<u>s</u>
pear<u>s</u>

Page 63 Watch out for "y!"

1 toy, 2 toy<u>s</u>; 1 story,
2 stor<u>ies</u>; 1 key, 2 key<u>s</u>;
1 penny, 2 penn<u>ies</u>

Page 63 Puzzling plurals

thief/thieves	man/men
sheep/sheep	tooth/teeth
child/children	mouse/mice

Page 64 Bear's playground

Bear plays, Bear catches,
Bear splashes, Bear fixes,
Bear draws

Page 65 Watch out for "y!"

I hurry. Joshua hurries.
I enjoy it. Dad enjoys it.
I try it. My dog tries it, too.

Page 66 Monkey mayhem

throw   throwing
catch   catching
make   making
count   counting
hide   hiding

Page 67 Magic spells

bakeing (baking)
gived (gave)
hopeing (hoping)
"Gave" doesn't follow the rule.

Page 68 Y verbs

dry drying dried
study studying studied
enjoy enjoying enjoyed
carry carrying carried

Page 68 Double up!

I hop I am hopping
I hopped

Solutions

Page 69 Playful penguins

stopping skidding running
flapping plodding hugging

stopped skidded ran
flapped plodded hugged

Page 70 Sight words

"When will you/he/she/we be
the same age as me/you?"

Page 71 Sight words

thay (they)
luve (love)

Page 72 Tricky words

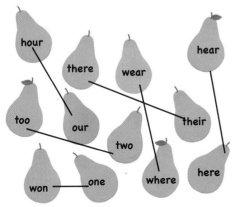

Page 73 Night knight

sea see bare bear
night knight hare hair
right write eight ate

Page 74 Jigsaw puzzle

board — keyboard
shine — sunshine
ground — playground
flake — snowflake
ball — basketball
fly — dragonfly
not — cannot

Page 75 Word builder

nowhere, nothing, somewhere,
sometime, something,
anywhere, anything, anyway,
anytime, everything,
everywhere

Page 75 What's the word?

caveman starfish
earthworm eyelid
friendship pancake

Page 76 Pick a spelling

apple coral animal cereal
bottle hospital middle tunnel little

Page 77 Follow the trails

gerbil	eagle	jackal	squirrel
pencil	tickle	petal	parcel
stencil	capital	double	barrel
nostril	puddle	vocal	chapel
gentle	April	angel	musical
evil	beetle	magical	jewel
fossil	plural	table	travel

Page 78 Attention!

nation, fiction, action,
subtraction, fraction, section,
petition, addition

Page 79 Complete the
sentences

The train stopped at the
station.
I love watching television.
The family lived in a mansion.
The wizard made a potion.
Do you want a portion of pie?

Solutions

Page 80 Clumsy clown

careful   care**less**

care**ful**   care**less**

Page 80 Suffix puzzle

These are some possible solutions: **helpless, sadness, enjoyment, tearful, slowly, painful**

Page 81 How do they do it?

You could have chosen any describing word (adverb).

Page 82 Word whales

Page 83 Dinosaur families

fast fast**er** fast**est**

fat   fat**ter**   fat**test**

cute cut**er** cut**est**

scary   scar**ier**   scar**iest**

Page 84 Sausage dogs

Page 85 Contrary Mary

It is. It is**n't!**
You did. I did**n't!**
You should. I should**n't!**
It has. It has**n't!**
You have. I have**n't**.